REVELATION
Unveiling the Mask

Precious A. Jackson

To Frank & Gran

"Live & Shine"

Precious Jackson

4/23/14

Revelation - Unveiling The Mask

Books may be purchased in quantity and/or special sales by contacting the publisher, Lady P. Productions, at (323) 451-9071, or by email at LadyPtheAuthor@gmail.com.

Published by Lady P. Productions
Interior Design by LaShawn Walls, iZiggy Promotions
Cover Design by Dynasty's Cover Me
Editing by LaShawn Walls, iZiggy Promotions and Gail Butler
ISBN: 978-0-692-22267-6
First Edition
Printed in USA

Contents

Foreword

In the opening stanza of his classic poem *We Wear the Mask*, Paul Lawrence Dunbar writes:

> We wear the mask that grins and lies,
> It hides our cheeks and shades our eyes,—
> This debt we pay to human guile;
> With torn and bleeding hearts we smile,
> And mouth with myriad subtleties.

This poem eloquently captures the temptation that we all struggle with to be honest about who we are in a world that does not value honesty. Instead of sharing our true feelings and opinions, we settle for what's popular and politically correct. We all pretend to be better than we are and act as though we have more wisdom than Solomon and more patience than Job. We fail to realize the power that is in our stories, and that we "overcome by the blood of the lamb and by the word of our testimony."(Revelation 12:11)

In the coming pages, you will read the story of a woman who has been delivered from shame, who has torn away the mask, and is courageous enough to share how God has moved her from strength to strength, faith to faith, and glory to glory. God has given Precious Jackson the precious gift of self-revelation—and as she holds the mirror up to herself, she helps all of us see ourselves better.

Pastor Joseph Carlos Robinson
Resurrection Church of Los Angeles

Acknowledgments

I would like to thank my Lord and Savior, Jesus Christ, for giving me the strength and the courage to write this book. This journey was not easy; God tugged at my spirit for a long time. Thank You, God, for your patience.

Thank you, my angels in heaven: my mother, Ernestine; my surrogate mother, Georgette; and my grandmother, Dessie; and thanks to my father, Percy. Each of you helped shape me into the woman that I am today. I cherish our candid conversations, your sound advice and the good and the bad times that we shared. I know that all of you all are watching over me from heaven. I feel your presence everywhere I go. Not a day goes by that I don't think about each of you.

Thanks to my inner circle, Markeisha, Alfredia, Robin and Yolanda for encouraging me, making suggestions as I wrote this book, and helping me cook and sell dinners to raise the money to finance this venture. I love you to pieces!

Thanks to my former coworkers at Women Alive who gave it to me straight, no chaser, when I was going through personal ordeals. Thank you, Corey, my friend and my brother, for never sugarcoating anything when it came to life.

Thanks to my coworkers and supervisors on the G-Floor at the Pasadena Public Health Department for giving me the support and time off that I needed to care for my daddy during his illness.

Thank you, family members, for never treating me differently because of my HIV-Positive status. Thank you, also, for your support and encouraging words when I decided to write this book.

Thank you, big brothers Michael and Ronald, for defending my honor no matter what. Thank you for always giving me sound advice on the subject of men.

Dedication

*To women everywhere who silently suffer
intimate partner violence.*

FULL FLIGHT
FROM REALITY

When I attended Narcotics Anonymous meetings with my surrogate mother who was in recovery—may she rest in peace—I used to hear people say, *"I was full flight from reality."* I didn't understand what it meant at the time until my friend Corey broke it down. WHEN YOU'RE IN A SOBER STATE OF MIND (AND THIS DOESN'T JUST APPLY TO PEOPLE WHO USE DRUGS AND ALCOHOL) AND YOU MAKE A CONSCIOUS DECISION TO ENGAGE IN BEHAVIORS THAT YOU KNOW WILL HAVE A NEGATIVE OUTCOME, YOU ARE FULL FLIGHT FROM REALITY!

THE BAD BOY (MY TYPE)

In June 2005, I was at work when I received a call from a guy named Trevon. He was calling to inquire about a support group that my agency provided for heterosexual men and women who were living with chronic illnesses. During that time in my life, I was grieving from the loss of my surrogate mother in 2004 and I was vulnerable. From the sound of Trevon's voice, I imagined him to be a tall, dark-skinned, sexy man; I just hoped he had all his teeth. Now, this is a potential client and I'm excited about meeting him although my company's policy stated clearly that employees were not allowed to date clients but I was willing to ignore the policy. That should have been a sign, a red flag, but I was full flight from reality.

Trevon's day to visit the office finally arrived. When he walked into the office, I knew that my mental image of the good looking man with that great sounding voice had been a fantasy. This scenario alone lets you know why we should leave our fantasies in La-La Land. Standing just 5'6" tall, this brown-skinned man was SHORT! I am not the tallest person in the world but I like my men to tower over my 5'5" height.

We walked toward the building where intake was conducted to assess a new client's needs which is outside of the main structure where the administration offices are housed and peer services such as emotional support groups and one-on-one counseling are provided. I asked Trevon the standard intake questions: *"Do you have a history of incarceration?"* *"Yes, I've spent the past twenty years of my life in and out of prison,"* he responded. My eyes began to glisten and I shifted in my seat. Trevon didn't know it, but I had a thing for thugged-out, gangsta niggas, especially if they had served time in jail or prison. Trevon may have not noticed, but as I got to know him, I became very excited. He was about to be my next victim; I'd made up in my mind that Trevon was the one for me and that we were about to start dating.

In my mind, Trevon was the man that I wanted him to be. I started dating Trevon in June. He dated me with love and respect and provided for my every need (yeah, right!). In July, Trevon moved all of his belongings into my place. Now if that's not full flight from reality, what is? Of course, there were some consequences for the act of dating a client—I was placed on a three-day leave without pay. Not only was I temporarily insane but I also had unresolved childhood abandonment issues stemming from my relationship with my birth mom. I always lived by the philosophy that if I am healthy and working then my man, if he is in good health, should also be employed. When I met Trevon all that shit went straight out the door. I was stuck with a man who was healthy and took care of his bills with Social Security

Supplemental Income (an SSI check). Who would've thought that I would go against my own philosophy? I must admit, Trevon had me spun in his web. I even went so far as to tag along with him when he told me we were moving because he had qualified for Section 8. Instead of me looking at him and telling him to get the hell on, all I could see was me saving money because the rent and utilities would be fully paid. Not only had Trevon been in prison, but he also had a history of substance abuse. With the exception of three men, every man that I ever dated or married was either a drug addict in recovery or had relapsed back into his familiar pattern of drug abuse.

DICKMATIZED

Trevon and I were making passionate love. My head was spinning through the entire lovemaking session. He was so good at pleasuring each and every part of my body—that sweet kind of lovemaking that will have you giving your man the keys to your car when you know good and damn well he doesn't have anything in his wallet except a state issued identification card. Trevon knew when to ask me for something and this night was no different. When he asked me for the keys to go get a beer, I didn't even answer. I just leaned over and pulled the keys out of my purse and handed them to him. Shit, the way he had just laid it on me, I almost felt like *I* needed a beer. When the sex is right, we tend to do anything for our man because we know he'll keep it coming; but this time, when Trevon drove away in my car, my world began to change in ways that I could never have imagined.

Three days pass and still no car and no Trevon. I knew that I was in trouble because I had been through similar situations with my ex-husband who was an addict and would leave for three or four days looking for his next fix. On the eve of the third night, with nothing else left to do, I fell on my knees and began to pray: *"God, I can't do this, I've been down this road before and I know in my heart that Trevon is using. I don't have the strength to deal with this or the drama that comes with it."* We all know that God answers prayers, but we must be careful what we ask for if we aren't ready to handle what He's going to put before us. After placing my troubles in the hands of the Lord, there was a knock at the door and guess who? Exactly. Trevon. He staggered through the door wearing different clothes and looking busted as ever; I knew then that he was using. *Baby, you are too good for me. I'm addicted to these streets and you deserve someone better than me,"* Trevon explained. When a man decides to bare his soul, which is not often, you'd better listen. It was God speaking to me and His voice came in the form of Trevon's and I needed to heed His warning. This was my scapegoat and it was up to me to either run before the pain and heartache kicked in or just sit back and enjoy the ride. Fear engulfed me as I began to think of all the lonely nights that were to come. I was still grieving over the passing of my surrogate mother and the thought of losing something that I had control over was not in my plan. *"Baby, please don't leave. We can work through this together"* are the words that rolled off my tongue signifying approval of Trevon's behavior and the drama that was yet to come…. Full flight from reality!

A HARD HEAD MAKES
A SOFT ASS

Deep down I knew that choosing to stay with Trevon was a big mistake but my yearning to be with someone caused me to make decisions that were not in my best interests. All I could see was me taking care of Trevon's needs and proving to him that I was not like the women in his past. Helping Trevon was a burden but I couldn't see that then. All of the women before me had sense enough to leave Trevon and his drug addicted behind.

Packing and moving out of my nice, peaceful, standalone, large one bedroom apartment in Inglewood, California which afforded me the luxury of plush, wall-to-wall carpeting, wood paneling throughout the dinette area, wood kitchen cabinetry and a large bay window through which sunrays bounced off my bluish grey walls was a radical change. As soon as we drove up to the building, I knew I wanted to return to my own habitat but to make Trevon happy, I smiled as I walked into my new, plain white-walled apartment with its thin carpeting, large bay window and as a featured amenity, a building that blocked the view. The apartment was two flights up in a twenty unit dump-plex on 110th Street between Budlong and Vermont in Los Angeles.

I hoped for a better outcome as a result of our move but Trevon resumed his drama filled lifestyle in less than twenty-four hours. Instead of taking our rented U-Haul truck back to the rental location, Trevon decided to haul it around the city on a hunt to quench his appetite for a fix. My blood was boiling. The U-Haul rental agency called me on my job to inform me that their truck was missing and I was pissed! I went straight home where I found Trevon lying face down in his own vomit. All I could do was shake my head at the sight of him. I was mad, but I was mostly angry at myself because I chose to stay in the relationship. Trying to fix Trevon was mostly about me being a co-dependent. I wanted to rescue Trevon from himself and make him into the man I wanted him to be. Nonetheless, because things weren't going the way I'd planned, I persecuted Trevon for his wrongdoings. I let him know how I felt when I got the call about the truck. *"You ain't shit but a stupid ass crackhead,"* I yelled. After making that statement, I had to ask myself, *"Who's really stupid here?"* I'm the one who made the decision to ride with this relationship. Trevon had given me my walking papers but once again, I gave them back.... Full flight from reality! To cover up Trevon's mess, my father-in-law and I went to the U-Haul location and said that the truck had been stolen. In order to make the lie official, the manager requested that we go to the local precinct and file a police report. Now, as you can see, co-dependents of an addicted person tend to fix and rescue. We have a tendency to cover up the mess. When we submit to their drama, an addict's problems become our problems.

Trevon and I married in September 2005 and I immediately began to believe that we could live a fairytale life. I really thought that things would be different. (NOT!) In my world, I envisioned a wedding night filled with passion as we consummated our special day. Instead, I was home alone. The phone rang at two o'clock in the morning. It was a collect call from Trevon. *"Baby! Can you come and pick me up from La Cienega and Venice? I don't have money and I don't have any shoes on,"* Trevon said. *"What happened to your shoes?"* I asked. *"I sold them for some crack,"* Trevon replied. All I could do was drop my head. When I left Trevon at his friend's house to finish celebrating *our* day, he was dressed to the nines. I had bought Trevon an expensive pair of shoes because I wanted my man to look good on our day. I even purchased our wedding rings because I wanted to make sure we had them.... So out of order! The chaos that occurred on our wedding day only scratched the surface. The coming months brought way more than I expected. Each month, Trevon received his SSI check and by the time I got home from work he'd be broke. I would cringe as I opened the door because I knew Trevon would be inside waiting to ask me for money. He would tell a convincing lie to get what he wanted. Because I didn't know how to stand up for myself by exhibiting tough love, I supported Trevon's habit by giving in. Submitting to Trevon was what I was supposed to do as a wife but I didn't feel good about the cycle of doing everything for Trevon and hoping for a different result. I was always supporting Trevon's habit while hoping that things would change. At that time in my life, I knew the situation wasn't going to change unless I changed but I wasn't ready. The sad part about it all is that I needed Trevon so that I could feel needed.

Trevon would go out some nights and be gone for a week leaving me to pace the floor and wonder where he was and if he was okay out there in the streets. I was as consumed with my own addiction (co-dependency) as Trevon was with his. My focus was not on myself, as it should have been, even though Trevon often left me stranded and I would have to catch the bus to work, or because of the humiliation I felt when I heard the words of a co-worker, who also was in recovery from drugs, when she reminded me that it doesn't get better, it gets worst. During that point in my life, I was depressed and consumed with anger. I was upset with myself for making the mistake of marrying Trevon. *Precious! You are so stupid! YOU SHOULD HAVE NEVER MARRIED TREVON! He's not married to you! He's married to crack! Look at you now, you're in a marriage all by yourself; you should've stayed single.* The one thing that I knew in my heart was that divorce was not an option. Divorcing Trevon would signify that my marriage failed and I couldn't let everyone know that I didn't have my life in order. After all, I had an image to protect. Everyone thought that Precious had it all together but I knew damn well that my life was fucked up.

A MOMENT OF CLARITY

They say the first thing to do is admit that, your life is in shambles and I did. When I admitted to myself that I was tired of all the hurt and chaos that my marriage was bringing, a light began the shine. One Saturday in October 2005 is a day that will always be embedded in my brain. I was going through a vicious cycle of co-dependency. Trevon was "on one"—antsy, discontent and *dis-eased!* He'd spent all of his money and his habit was starting to spill over into our household finances, not to mention, *my* purse. Instead of dealing with Trevon's dramatics, I went to the grocery store and wrote a check over the amount of the purchase so that I could get cash back to tide me over until I received my paycheck. That same night I came home from a children's event that I attended with my nieces and Trevon was waiting for me as I entered the door. I could tell by his behavior that he'd been using but he still asked to use my car to go over to his homie's house. Now let me remind you, I did say this man had been using all day. I knew because I was the one who gave him the money to cop some drugs and at that very moment, he was tweaking. Trying to be rational, I attempted to convince Trevon not to go anywhere since we hadn't spent any time together. Just picture me, a woman who has never used drugs a day in her life standing in front of a person who is irrational and addicted to crack and trying to have a rational conversation. Being the master manipulator that he was, Trevon convinced me to let him use the car. He promised that he would be right back. As he walked out of the door, I yelled, *"Please come back tonight because you know I have to go to work on Monday."* In my heart, I knew he wasn't coming right back because having my car gave him the motivation he needed to stay out for four or five days like he always did. I still didn't have the courage not to let him go.

Sunday came and I decided to do some chores around the house. I popped in a video and listened to Bishop Noel Jones. My spirit weighed on me heavily and I felt convicted about the night before. That was when I knew something was wrong with me. My inner spirit began to speak to me and it was something fierce: *Precious! What is wrong with you? How can you let that man continuously talk you into letting him use your car and you know he's going to get drugs and stay out for three days!* For me, this was my moment of clarity. You see, Trevon was not the only one with a problem; I had a problem as well. I allowed God to open my eyes and let me see my own reflection. I could hear the women at the Co-Dependents Anonymous (CoDA) meetings bearing witness about how they were able to build up their self-esteem by putting themselves first and knowing their own self-worth. I could hear one lady telling her story loud and clear. She spoke about how she put her life on the back burner to support her husband's addiction. She covered up for him if he missed work. She lost her own identity because she was so focused on taking care of his problems and his needs. Her last statement was powerful and it resonates in my mind to this day: *"I'm tired of getting the LAST end of the stick!"* At that very moment, I could feel those words building me up. I, too, was tired of being tired. I made the decision to pack my bags and leave my drug-filled life.

THE MOVE

The day that I moved out validated what I'd heard at the CoDA meetings. It was all so clear to me now: I am VALUABLE. I am IMPORTANT. I need to start putting my needs before those of others. All of that was true; I was worth more than all the hurt and pain inflicted on me by someone who did not embody the strength to carry himself, let alone to support me. With each box I packed, I encouraged myself toward greatness: *"Girl, you are doing the right thing because this is the first time you have ever even thought of putting your needs first and do what's best for you."* At the same time, I started feeling guilty because I had promised Trevon that I would never leave him. Now, my emotions had me questioning my own judgment. I wondered what Trevon was going to do without me; who was going to take care of him when I left? It's hard to deal with your own emotions when you allow the best interests of someone else to cloud your judgment. As humans, we sometimes think that people need us to take care of them when in actuality they don't. You see, Trevon never really needed me. He didn't need me to help him buy drugs or alcohol. He didn't need me when he first walked into the intake center where I worked. The truth is, Trevon just wanted someone to indulge his habits. Instead of drowning in my fear, I decided to accept the fact that if I removed myself from Trevon's life his mother would pick up what remained of her child and begin to nurture Trevon back to the man she raised him to be.

Unbeknownst to Trevon, my moving date had been scheduled for a Saturday in November 2005 and I was ready to move forward with my life. Trevon pulled up just as I was moving the last box out of the house we shared—just in time to see the truck filled with boxes and my car filled with the trophies of my life. Trevon went ballistic. *"Bitch, I don't need you! I got my homies and they got my back!"* He could be heard throughout the neighborhood. I spat out a few obscenities myself but I knew at that moment that I was doing the right thing by leaving Trevon. For the first time in my life, I was in control. However, moving away from my life with Trevon meant going back to life with a man for whom I still felt resentment—my father. I was embarrassed about moving in with my dad and there were issues from the past that he and I needed to work through.

I am a woman who marches to the beat of her own drum. Now, I felt like a caged animal. As soon as I stood under my father's roof I felt the weight of his rules and regulations: What time to be in at night; what time the kitchen closes; what time must the lights go out. I was on edge but I promised myself that I would do my best to make the situation work, and by the grace of God, it did! Our relationship strengthened itself. My dad provided valuable insight about how relationships were supposed to be. I loved the moments that we shared, but after two months, I felt like it was time to move. Trevon and I had started speaking again. He'd checked himself into a drug program to help him get back on track, but in retrospect, I think he only did so because he knew that I wanted him to get it together and that I wanted my marriage to work.

While Trevon was repairing and rebuilding himself, I needed to do the same. I started attending Tough Love, a self-help support group for families and friends of alcoholics and addicts that is an extension of the drug and alcohol program, Free-N-One. I really needed guidance to overcome what I endured in my marriage. I was still not ready to work a twelve steps program. Deep down, I felt that if Trevon would let go of his addiction to crack, everything would be great between us. Now that I see things clearly, I realize that I didn't recognize my own addiction as a co-dependent. I too, needed to be free—free from rescuing and taking care of needy people who always played the victim role—but because I was still broken, I immediately went back to rescuing Trevon. One day I received a phone call from Trevon out of the blue. He said he needed some toiletries, clothes, shoes and other items because he was being transferred to the Acton Drug Program in Antelope Valley. Back then, drug rehabilitation facilities had discretionary funds to provide basic necessities to indigent clients. As his wife, I felt obligated to provide for Trevon nonetheless. I went shopping and purchased everything he asked for. It felt good to be doing things for my husband again and I truly believed that Trevon was trying to recover and save our marriage, or so I thought. Seeing Trevon for the first time in two months made my heart skip a beat. We were both excited about reconnecting. It was as if we were meeting for the first time. We laughed and talked about how we ended up in that place in that moment. Trevon apologized to me for his actions and asked me if I would consider coming back home after he completed the program. Of course, I said yes; while I wanted more than anything in the world to save us, what motivated me even more was the opportunity to save face with outsiders, especially my peers. I wanted to prove to them that I, Precious A. Jackson was not a failure.

ROCK BOTTOM

Trevon left his drug rehabilitation program in January 2006 after committing to sixty days of sobriety. I moved back in with him and we were working on rebuilding our marriage. At first, it was like paradise. We spent quality time together and enjoyed each other's company. We went places together like couples do. For a moment, Trevon truly went the extra mile but once he realized that he was back at home and had the freedom to do what he wanted, Trevon relapsed and his drug addiction escalated to an even higher level than before. He resumed his pattern of stealing. Whenever I left home for overnight business, Trevon would steal anything and everything in the house. First it was the television. Then the stereo system. Eventually, most of my household items were sold on the street for drugs and there was no way for me to retrieve them. I was not operating in the spirit but in the flesh. I continuously fell for Trevon's manipulating ways. I continued to allow him to use my car knowing good and damn well that I wouldn't see my car until a week later when the gas light was on. It should be obvious that I was FULL FLIGHT FROM REALITY! I found myself back in full stress mode.

I was sitting at my desk one Monday in February 2006. My body was there but my mind was somewhere else. I was going through the motions of reading and responding to emails but I couldn't comprehend a word of what I read. I felt like my spirit had risen from my chair and left my body. I was so stressed out that I didn't notice that my co-worker, Araceli was peeping into my work zone. Apparently, she knew that something was wrong. Araceli approached me and suggested that we talk. Ordinarily, I don't share my problems with co-workers, but when Araceli asked me what was wrong, the floodgates opened and the details of my situation poured out of my mouth and into her ears. Araceli listened to me without saying a word. She wasn't judgmental nor did she offer opinions or advice; she just provided the emotional support I needed. Araceli and I weren't just co-workers, we were great friends and had been for years. She's been like a sister to me. We don't sugarcoat anything with each other. If Araceli needs support of any type, I got her and she reciprocates. Ladies, I don't care if you are single, in a relationship or married, always maintain a support network because heaven forbid, if your partner decides to leave one day, God and your sistah friends will still be there. Araceli and I spoke frequently about my life with Trevon and she always advised me to leave him but I wasn't ready at that time. I had already begun the process of cleansing and renewing Precious, so on that day, February 6, 2006, I decided that enough was enough and I was going to give Trevon an ultimatum—terms that he would have to agree to if he wanted to keep me in his life. This time it wouldn't be me who moved out. I would change the locks on Trevon's Section 8 apartment door and put him out. After all, I was the one who paid the bills. This time, I wanted Trevon to feel what it's like to be put out of his home and locked out of a relationship with someone who had his back, gave him money and supported his habit.

I left work that day on a new mission to take back my life. I stopped at Home Depot and purchased new locks and went home to lock Trevon's behind out, but as life would have it, Trevon had other plans for me. When I pulled into the driveway, Trevon was outside talking to his boys and some of the other neighborhood nobodies. They routinely sat around planning what they were going to do once their wives or girlfriends got home from work with their cars. In my opinion, if all of them got off their asses and got a job, they could have their own cars to do what they wanted, but who was I to talk. Anyway, Trevon walked over to the car, and if looks could kill, Trevon's mama would soon be planning his funeral. One look at me and Trevon clearly understood that I wasn't in the mood for his bullshit. I just rolled my eyes and pulled inside the gate. All I wanted to do was relax and that's just what I was planning to do. I went upstairs, changed my clothes and lay down on the couch. I knew I only had a few minutes before Trevon entered the house to beg me for something or come in just to babble on about what he wanted to do for the evening in my car. The house had been quiet and peaceful for all of fifteen minutes when Trevon came through the door. What transpired next was far from what I could ever imagine. Trevon's anger had escalated to another level and his addiction was eating him from the inside out. To this day, I sit and wonder what would've happened if I had done a Tyler Perry/Madea and took my earrings off. As I waited for a moment to exhale, Trevon came in and immediately invaded my space. He walked around to the side of the couch where I was lying and slapped my face so hard that my glasses flew across the room. Before I could get my bearings, Trevon grabbed my neck and started choking me. He had evolved into the devil in the flesh. As I gasped for air I began to pray to God asking Him to let me live. I didn't want to die like that and I knew God could protect me from all hurt, harm and evil. Trevon choked me for what seemed like ten minutes before releasing my neck. He must have seen the color leaving my face and my lips turning blue because the expression that was on his face when he first started choking me had turned into disbelief. I sat up on the couch coughing and choking as I tried to get oxygen into my lungs and brain. I didn't know what was coming next, so I tried to gain as much energy as possible before Trevon made his next move. I was shocked and terrified at the same time. I couldn't believe that this man had just put his hands on me. Trevon appeared to have gained his composure, but he continued to talk shit. *"You disrespected me outside in front of my homeboys. Do you know who the fuck I am? Just in case you forgot, I am Scorpio from Mafia Gangsta Crips (MGC)."* Now, this nigga knew good and damn well that he may have been

Scorpio from MGC back in the day, but at that moment, he was Scorpio the crackhead and I wasn't putting anything past him. I knew he was crazy but I didn't know that Trevon had gone all the way off the Richter scale. But on the real, at that moment, I was intimated by him. I didn't know what was going to happen next and Trevon knew he had my full attention and he played on my emotions. Trevon threatened to whoop my ass if I didn't get him some money. *"I don't give a damn how you have to get me money, but you better get it,"* he yelled at the top of his lungs. You know how they say God works in mysterious ways? Well, this was one of His mysterious moments. I routinely left my debit card at work because Trevon had started stealing money and anything else in my purse that appeared to be of any value to support his habit. To prevent him from coming to my job and potentially causing a scene, Trevon and I always went to a check cashing location for me to take out payday loans. Unfortunately, since I had an outstanding loan, on that particular day, I couldn't get another one. I knew that I was going to have to do something to keep myself out of harm's way. Trevon was furious as hell because I couldn't get a loan and was cursing before we got back into the car. He got behind the wheel and sped out of the check cashing place, driving erratically, pushing the pedal to the floor then suddenly slamming on the brakes. At my breaking point and afraid out of my mind, I gave in and told Trevon to take me to my job to get my debit card. I was hoping that no one would see me walk into the building because I didn't know if the hand marks from being choked by the man I loved still appeared on my face or neck. As luck would have it, one of the licensed clinical social workers was conducting a group session and happened to look up and see the fear and trauma on my face. She excused herself from her group and asked if I was okay. Since I didn't know what Trevon would do next, I just told her that I had gotten into an argument with my husband because we had to drive all the way back to my job to get my debit card and that he was outside in the car and I didn't want to keep him waiting.

I wanted so badly to tell my co-worker about my situation but fear was rising in me and I just needed for this to be over with. I began to hyperventilate as I walked back to the car. We headed to the closest ATM machine which happened to be in a CVS Pharmacy across from my job. Trevon got out of the car and went inside with me. I knew that he did so to make sure that I didn't pull any stunts. As I made the transaction, Trevon hovered over my shoulders and pressed his pointing finger into my back like it was a gun. I was sick to my stomach; it was as if Trevon had forgotten that I was his wife. He was treating me like I was just another person off the street. He didn't care that I was about to withdraw my last three hundred and twenty dollars from the bank which was that month's payment on the car that he so loved to drive. All Trevon could think about was his next fix.

On the way home all I could think about was what was

going to happen when we arrived. Was Trevon satisfied now that he had money and was about to take my car or was he going to take things to a physical level and hurt me again? I was traumatized by the entire series of events. I just couldn't believe that Trevon would take things this far. When we pulled up in front of the house I didn't know if I was supposed to get out or wait for him. He looked over at me and told me to get out. I go out and slowly walked toward the house. Before I went inside I turned to look at my license plate to make sure that I knew the plate number from memory. I walked into the house and went straight to the bedroom. I sat in the middle of the bed, still in disbelief, trying to figure out what my next move should be. I telephoned Darlene, a friend and co-worker who was a former drug and alcohol abuser who had been clean and sober for twelve years. Darlene knew about the situation between Trevon and myself and constantly warned me that Trevon's relapses were going to get progressively worse. I talked to Darlene and told her what had just gone down. She informed me that Trevon's actions constituted armed robbery and that I needed to file a police report. I hung the up phone and dropped to my knees. I began to have a conversation with God. *"Lord, if I stay here, then I'm dead, spiritually, emotionally and most likely physically, but if I leave, I can live."* There was no doubt in my mind that I wanted to live. I got up off my knees and started packing the biggest duffle bag I could find. I packed every square inch of the bag with my belongings and went to my neighbor's house. I explained what had transpired and asked if she would take me to the police station and then to my best friend's house.

Fear didn't leave me when I left the house. My next challenge was to convince a deputy sheriff in Lennox, California that Trevon had actually done me harm. I'd heard stories about how women who attempt to report intimate partner violence (IPV) sometimes aren't taken seriously and the intake officer refuses to file a report. After standing in line for fifteen minutes, Officer White called me to the desk. I will never forget Officer White because he showed compassion and took my complaint seriously. Officer White genuinely was there to serve and protect. All I could say was, *thank you God*, for He truly answered my prayers. I began to cry hysterically as I described to Officer White what had occurred. Officer White asked me to calm down, take several deep breaths and continue with my story. Calming myself, I described every detail as I if it were happening at that very moment. After I had provided all of the traumatic details of the day's events, Officer White took photographs of the now swollen and red handprint on the left side of my face where Trevon slapped me. No one will ever know how grateful I am for Officer White's kindness and concern. I'd never had a negative experience but based on what I'd seen and heard about police brutality and racial profiling against Black men and women, there's no doubt in mind that Officer White epitomizes the concept of serving and protecting.

Too often, women get into trouble because we make decisions based on emotions and not facts. If, for example, you are in a relationship where the dude is emotionally and verbally abusive and causes you to be fearful and to feel worthless but you continue to stay, then you are giving your abuser the greenlight to continue the abuse which may result in more physical harm or even death. If you are currently in a physically and emotionally volatile relationship, take time to pray and mediate on this verse: *The Lord is a refuge for the oppressed, a stronghold in times of trouble.* (Psalm 9:9-10) Many women with children don't realize that by being in a relationship that involves intimate partner violence, they are teaching their children a negative image of how a woman should be treated. Children learn what they live. If a boy sees a man beating on his mother, that boy may grow into a man who believes he should hit a woman. If a girl sees a man hitting her mother, that girl may grow into a woman who considers male-inflicted violence appropriate behavior.

SAFETY ZONE

After making the police report, I called one of my best friends, Marsha, and went to her house. I told Marsha what had happened and that I needed a place to lay low for a while. Although Trevon knew a lot about me, he never knew where Marsha resided. For some reason, I never took him to her house and I was glad because her home became a safe haven for me to escape all the madness. Since Trevon knew where my other best friend Alfredia lived, I didn't want to chance going there and bringing drama to her doorstep. After settling in at Marsha's, I decided to call other friends to let them know what had happened and most importantly, to let them know that I was safe. Since it had been a while since I spoke with Alfredia, I knew that conversation was going to take some time. I'd been avoiding having conversations with Alfredia because I didn't want her to judge me for making the poor decision to get back with Trevon and try to repair our broken marriage. Having good friends is one of the best things in the world; they always know when something is wrong with you. Alfredia knew that my life was in turmoil. She told me that she had already prayed for me because she felt in her spirit that something was wrong and that had I come to her earlier, she would not have passed judgment. I was relieved that she understood my predicament which let me know that I didn't have to feel guilty for not calling her over the past few months. Alfredia is one of those friends that you talk with on the telephone for hours every day and spend your spare time at work texting about anything and everything.

While my conversation with Alfredia went smoothly, when I informed my father of what had transpired with Trevon, he was visibly upset. Later, I found out just how upset he was. My father called some of his associates who were still running the streets and they went to the house looking to pay Trevon a visit for putting his hands on me. I felt all warm inside to know that my dad was ready and willing to protect his daughter. He told me that he was glad I was safe and that his door was always open to me.

That experience with Trevon was a nightmare of unconventional proportions. I couldn't believe that this shit was happening to me. How did I become a victim of domestic violence? Since I always defended Trevon for his actions, I never realized that I was experiencing verbal and emotional abuse the entire time that we were together. Denial in intimate relationships seemed to be a pattern for me. I remember dealing with the same type of abuse from a guy that I dated eleven years ago. As the saying goes, *if you don't learn the lesson you are doomed to repeat it.* For me, each relationship began with smiles and kind gestures and evolved into verbal confrontations where I endured name calling, reprimanding, isolation from my friends and family, and last but not least, physical abuse—all red flags—but I was so caught up in having and keeping a man that I didn't want to recognize the signs. I didn't know how to love myself; I subjected myself to abuse because I believed that even if there were good men, I was unworthy. I would say to myself, *"Niggas ain't shit, and besides, there are no good men left."* Since I kept telling myself that, what kind of men do you think I attracted? Bingo! Men who were as emotionally broken as I was. I justified staying with Trevon based on our mutual circumstances: (1) Like myself, Trevon was HIV positive and I understood the challenges associated with living with a chronic illness; (2) the dick was good; (3) when he was sober, Trevon had a sense of humor; and (4) I loved him.

Staying at Marsha's house afforded me a safe environment in which to regroup but I needed to figure out what my next steps were going to be. I was still holding down my job but I had to take the bus to work. Trevon had taken my car and the police hadn't found it yet. There were things that I had done that just didn't line up with who I was. I'd allowed Trevon to change me in many ways. For example, I grew my hair out just to please him. I had always worn my hair short; for me to change that feature after so many years was an indication that I was losing my self-worth. Now, for the first time in a very long time, I was about to regain my strength. Making an appointment and having my hair cut short renewed my self-confidence and put me on a journey toward recovery. I was molding a new and improved Precious; I was ready to take on the world with my newfound power. Thank you, Jesus, for new beginnings!

THE INTERVIEW

Two weeks after my traumatic ordeal with Trevon and my decision to reshape my life, blessings began to pour in. I was contacted by the producers of Black Entertainment Television (BET) who wanted to interview me for their news special, *Down Low Exposed,* a show that exposes the secret world of men who have sex with men while masquerading as heterosexuals and gambling with the lives of their female partners. I was curious to know how BET found me. The young lady who called said that she Googled "HIV positive women" and my name came up. I was ecstatic about the opportunity and I told her that it would be an honor to be interviewed. I was excited and proud of myself for doing what I said I would do—tell my story whether it was in print, media or up close and personal—in the hope that other women will never have to walk in my shoes. When my family read my story they were very proud of me for taking a positive, proactive approach to a situation that many people view as negative while also being of service to others. I was working at Women Alive when a journalist called from the *Washington Post* called to request an interview regarding Black women and HIV. I damn near died. I was excited and nervous at the same time because the *Washington Post* is a prestigious national newspaper and at that time there weren't any Black women that I knew of who were open about their HIV status. By the time *Newsweek* asked to interview me, I had been advocating for HIV Positive women locally and nationally for some time and I had become comfortable with being interviewed and confident that I was doing the right thing by getting the HIV prevention message out to Black women. I'm not boasting; those were opportunities that God blessed me with since I made a commitment to tell my story and educate people by any means necessary. What I didn't realize was that I had surrendered to the purpose that God had for my life.

During the BET interview, I told my truth and my perception of the things that had happened to me. I've always admitted that I had questioned the sexuality of the guy who infected me all along. I always felt that he was bisexual but I wasn't sure. His choice of positions always caused me to wonder. He was more interested in having anal sex than vaginal. It struck me as odd because I had never known a straight man who was so interested in having anal sex. I didn't submit to his suggestions or preferences because that wasn't my cup of tea. The BET news special aired in February 2006 and I must say, I didn't look like what I had been through. Baby, God is the only one I know that can redeem time. The day after the special aired, I was talking to my Executive Director at Women Alive and she said it would be nice if Bill Duke contacted us to do something on HIV and women. Mr. Duke was interviewed on the same BET news special as I was. It is something when you put things out in the universe and God answers your request and He did just that. The following week a producer representing Mr. Duke contacted Women Alive about participating in his documentary, *Faces*. I was floored. I did a dance for the Lord because I was awestruck by the opportunities that God was blessing me with. Women Alive agreed to participate and a week later, our little office (which was actually a house on Burnside Avenue in Los Angeles [we've moved from there since then]) was turned into a movie set. It was awesome! Not only did Mr. Duke write a documentary, he also wrote and directed a movie titled *Covered* about a woman who learned of her husband's closeted sexual preference when she caught him in the shower with a man. Ladies, if you are dating a man in the current millennium, there are things that you MUST know about him: (1) His credit score; (2) his criminal history; and (3) his sexual reproductive health history which means that both of you should undergo a battery of tests for sexually transmitted diseases (STDs), Human Immunodeficiency Virus (HIV) and Human Papillomavirus (HPV). Also, take heed to certain red flags:

Does he respect his mother and other females in his family? If not, likely he will likely not respect and treat you well.

Does he exhibit a pattern of saying that he's going to call you and neglecting to do so? If so, that's an indication that you are not a priority in his life. Don't be quick to submit to a man's needs before getting to know him.

Maintain high standards. Never compromise your self-worth for any man. Make him wait for sex.

THE TALK

In April 2006, I left my best friend's home and moved back in with my father. I wasn't thrilled about going back to my dad's but I needed to feel the comfort of home. I was going through a very emotional time and staying at my best friend's house seemed to be a problem. Her children were very uncomfortable having me there because of my HIV status. I had been coming around them for years and not once had they demonstrated negativity toward me; perhaps living with me was different for them than having me over as a guest. Unless people are forced to walk in an HIV-Positive person's shoes they will never understand the myths, the truths and the hurt that accompany that diagnosis.

The police finally found my car. I followed all the procedures and went to the impound lot to identify it. I hoped to find everything intact and functioning but regrettably, there was a hole where the radio had been snatched out, the rear window was broken, and the car was filled with trash but it wasn't as bad as it looked. I put my car in the shop for repairs and in less than a week it looked like new. THANK GOD FOR CAR INSURANCE!

After everything that I'd been through, by the time I

moved back in with my dad I had the courage to want and accept the help that I needed to build a new life. I attended a Tough Love meeting one night where a woman shared her experience of being in a co-dependent relationship. She made a profound statement: *"How dare we tell someone else what not to do, when it is their choice to do it."* That's when the error of my ways hit me like a ton of bricks: I tried to control Trevon by thinking that I could get him to stop abusing drugs by yelling, screaming and nagging him about his problem. Trevon's problems were a result of the choices he made. My role in our marriage was to take care of Precious by admitting to myself that I could not change Trevon or remove him from his situation. What I could've done early on was to separate myself from the unnecessary drama that accompanied Trevon's life. At that moment, I knew I was ready for my new beginning. I was also anxious to attend more Tough Love and CoDA meetings. Both are twelve step self-help fellowship programs for men and women whose common goal is to develop healthy relationships. I started attending church, bible study and self-help meetings regularly and gradually gained the strength and courage that I needed to begin the healing process. Poor decision-making had caused me to suffer hurt, pain, guilt and shame in unhealthy relationships. For a significant portion of my adult life, Precious Ann Jackson did not have her own personality; she was what everyone else wanted her to be. I hadn't trusted my own ideas and I based my life on other people's opinions. It wasn't until I began to digest the Word of God and to listen to what He thought of me that I began to come into my own as a person. I had to learn that I am valuable, loveable, worthy of good things, and that I am a beautiful person inside and out.

I knew God was working in my life when Trevon called me on Saturday, May 5, 2006 and said that he wanted to talk to me. Instantly, I hoped that he wanted to discuss getting back together because I missed him. In actuality, I was missing the good times we shared and not thinking about what I would have to compete with for Trevon's affection—namely, his addiction to crack. I was also Trevon's problem because I kept enabling him, thereby allowing my competition (drugs and alcohol) to win. Trevon's timing was perfect. I was in Victoria's Secret shopping for new underwear. He asked me to meet with him and I agreed. I felt giddy inside. I'd been waiting a long time for this moment. When I arrived at the designated meeting place, the Chesterfield Square Shopping Center on Slauson and Western, it was obvious that Trevon was as excited as I was. But for the fact that we'd hooked up at the Snooty Fox just a week earlier, this could've been like a first date. (If you're from Los Angeles you know which motel that is.) In any event, that hookup continues to be a lasting memory for me because it was the last time that I would ever be intimate with Trevon. Trevon and I walked around the shopping center parking lot for about two hours talking about his addiction and how far gone he had been. I had so many questions that deserved answers. I even asked Trevon if I had ever asked him for a hit of crack would he had given it to me. He replied, *"Yes, I would have."* That conversation was deeper than any that we'd ever had. I admitted to Trevon that I contributed to his addiction by co-signing his bullshit—helping him buy dope; manipulating him into believing that I was going to call his parole officer; and trying to fix and rescue him from himself. I explained to Trevon that my challenge was just as difficult as his because I didn't want to accept the part I played in the demise of our relationship yet I always blamed him for our separation. I no longer felt desirable, wanted or needed and because of Trevon's addiction, I no longer desired to be with him. In fact, I'd become so emotionally detached from Trevon that I was the one who put a stop to having sex with him. I knew God was in the conversation when Trevon said *"We need to get a divorce. I don't deserve a woman like you and you deserve a man who is going to treat you like a queen."* Trevon would have never said that on his own; the Holy Spirit was speaking through him and guess what? I didn't try to talk him out of it. I was through because I knew God was in the mix. We hugged and went our separate ways.

PURGING

I received a collect call from Trevon in the middle of May 2006. He called to inform me that he had been picked up by the police who discovered that his parole officer had issued a warrant for his arrest. Trevon was in the early stages of his recovery from drug abuse and not all of his character defects had fallen off. He was sweet talking me and telling me how much he still loved me and trying to insinuate that the system was trying to railroad him. Short and sweet, Trevon wanted me to drop the charges against him. The little girl in me felt sorry for him. My conscious was eating away at me, reminding me that I was the person who called the police on Trevon. My emotions got the best of me and I headed to the courthouse. Now, when God is in control, you will always discover that He is working for the greater good. My bubble burst when I got to the courthouse. The clerk informed me that once the District Attorney picks up the case, the charges can no longer be dropped. Thanks to O.J. Simpson, California don't play that, homie! I can't say that I was upset by this turn of events because deep down, I didn't want to drop the charges. I wanted to be free and break the cycle of unhealthy relationships.

Like clockwork, Trevon called me the next day to follow up on his request to be released from jail. I informed him of the applicable law and told him there was nothing I could do since the case was now in the hands of the District Attorney. His next reaction was his best reaction: He went into his tantrums and called me every name in the book. At that moment I knew that he wasn't working to better himself, that this was just another plot to manipulate me into doing something for him. We argued back and forth. I was convinced that my original decision to leave Trevon to better myself was the right decision. Trevon really needed to get his life together. After becoming exhausted with his arguing, I hung up the phone in Trevon's face and I've never spoken to him again. At first, I felt apprehensive about my choice to let go, so I decided to get some old school advice from my dad and he confirmed that I had made the right decision.

The court date for my domestic violence case against Trevon arrived. My father went with me. I was so nervous that my hands wouldn't stop shaking and perspiring. I internalized my anxiety with my own self-proclaimed speech. *"Precious, you must separate your feelings from the facts! Trevon disrespected you verbally and emotionally and he has abused you physically. You are doing the right thing! This is about you loving yourself and taking care of you."* When Trevon entered the courtroom, my heart started beating a mile a minute. I grabbed my father's hand and told him that my nerves were getting the best of me. My father comforted me by telling me that everything was going to be fine and that he would walk with me every step of the way. As I looked around the courtroom, I could hear the muffled voices of everyone around me, but no sound was as clear as my own heartbeat. They called Officer White to the stand to give his account of what he witnessed. *"Let the show begin,"* I thought.

They called my name after what seemed like an eternity. I stood up and began praying as I walked to the witness stand. I needed God to be my co-pilot. With God in your life, all things are possible. God showed up and enabled me to deliver my account of what happened. I kept my composure and when it was time for me to be cross examined by Trevon's attorney I was able to stand and deliver. When Trevon's lawyer tried to question my credibility, my father got up from his seat and made his way to the swinging doors that led to the defense and plaintiff's tables. I knew that he was upset by the defense attorney's line of questioning, but until that moment, I didn't know just how upset my father was. *"Sir, what are you doing? Can you sit down?"* the judge said. *"I needed to stretch my legs,"* my father replied. Without a further word from anyone, the defense rested its case.

My dad and I were told to wait outside in the lobby until all of the witnesses had testified. I was curious to know why my dad had made a scene in the courtroom. *"Daddy, why did you get up while I was testifying?"* I asked. My dad responded, *"After listening to what that boy did to you and seeing those pictures, I was about to beat that little nigga's ass with my cane."* My dad was dead serious. Had the judge not stopped him, my dad would've knocked Trevon out. No one really knew the harsh reality of what I was dealing with. I told them and they speculated, but the pictures told a more gruesome story than any testimony.

As we were waiting to be called back into the courtroom, Officer White pushed through the heavy set of doors and saw us sitting in the designated area. He walked over and thanked me for coming to court. He told us that so many women don't show up after they file a report because they are too scared to testify against the perpetrator. I thanked Officer White for coming to my rescue, but I couldn't help feeling some kind of way when he walked off. I had heard the stories, but to hear it from an official makes it really sad. If you're a woman reading this and you're in a physically abusive relationship, please make a plan of escape and implement it safely. Explore your options; seek a place where your partner cannot find you and most importantly, file a police report and show up for court. You never know who can help you, but in my situation, I found out a week later when the detective called me that Trevon pleaded "no contest" and the court imposed a guilty verdict. Trevon was convicted of use of a deadly weapon resulting in physical harm and sentenced to ten years in prison. The following week I received the good news that Trevon would be out of my life for the next ten years. I went back to the courthouse with a sense of relief and filed for divorce. It was well worth $325 to be rid of Trevon. The filing process was very simple. I thank God that we didn't have any children or joint property.

In spite of all the commotion in my life, I continued

to work with Yvette, my Tough Love sponsor and had just finished the Third Step of the Twelve Steps program. *"We decided to turn our will and lives over to God through Jesus Christ, as well as to entrust our friends and family members to Him."* (Romans 10:9, Matthew 11:28-29, Matthew 16:25, 1Peter 5:7 and Proverbs 3:5.) Those bible verses helped me to understand that without God's help, I would continue to follow my own path and to make wrong decisions and remain stuck in relationships that weren't lasting. I couldn't change other people. They would have to change themselves in relationship with our Creator, just as I was doing.

Learning to follow His word revealed to me that I could no longer lean on my own understanding; I had to lean on what was spoken into my life. Our gut feelings and that small voice that speaks to us is God's way of keeping us safe from hurt, harm and danger. I was running off self-will and not His guidance. Throughout my adult life, I allowed my emotions to rule my decision-making. Everything I did was based on feelings, not facts. To this day, I can still hear one of my friends saying, *"Feelings aren't always facts."* I always wondered what Elizabeth meant when she said that. She was a dear friend in my HIV support group and a co-worker. Elizabeth is no longer with us, but I now know what she meant. My feelings had me tripped up because I wasn't removing my emotions and thinking about the situations rationally. These are things that I overlooked when I was seeking Precious. When you are trying to fix and rescue others to meet your own needs, if that effort is not driven by God, there will always be the possibility of a head-on collision. Of course, I can "go on one" sometimes and even though God has equipped me with knowledge, I'm not always willing to apply it. Fortunately, I now recognize when I'm getting in my own way.

I met with my Tough Love sponsor, Yvette, weekly to discuss my writing assignments. Now, this was not a program requirement—each sponsor's approach is different—but Yvette wanted me to write. I found writing to be therapeutic because I was able to see my feelings before me. I could acknowledge the roles that I played which helped me to see and change my thinking patterns and remove unhealthy behaviors. Yvette was always transparent in sharing how each step that we covered affected her. She shared how releasing pain, resentment and unforgiving ways helped her get to the naked truth about herself. I could see all of this coming together for me and I was super excited to move on to my next assignment, Step Four: *We asked God to help us make an inventory of ourselves that we might gain understanding.* Yvette warned me that I would need to lay everything on the table—all my hurt and resentment against anyone and how I played a part in it all. I was scared, but I wanted to know why I kept choosing the same men, why I was always getting the short end of the stick, and why I kept allowing people to use and abuse me. I prayed, *"Lord, please reveal the outcomes of this assignment. I know that if it's Your will, then it shall be done."* All I could do was cry out loud and wonder why I kept doing the things that I continued to do. I no longer wanted to make the same mistakes over and over again. As

I drove home from my sponsor's house I banged my hands on the steering wheel and I asked God to remove all the baggage that I had carried over the years. As soon as I got home, I wanted to wash away all negative energy and start anew. I took a bath and as I was walking into my bedroom God revealed what He wanted me to write about: *"I want you to start with your childhood, your abandonment issues, your avoidance of confrontations with authority figures, and your need to fix and rescue people."* This was God's revelation to me about me, about Precious Ann Jackson who didn't think she had any problems or issues, but who thought that everyone else had problems.

5/17/06 – 4th Step

We asked God to help us make an inventory of ourselves that we might gain understanding.

Childhood Issues

Abandonment - *At 9 years of age when my parents stopped coming to pick me up on the weekends I felt alone, like they didn't want me anymore. Also when I turned 13 years of age, I found out that Georgette was not my biological mother, but Ernestine was my maternal mother. She told my father to come get me. When I heard that I felt like my mother just threw me away. What was wrong with me that she didn't want me? Why would she do that to her child? This is when I started becoming really clingy to people because I wanted to belong, to be part of someone or something. I felt rejected by my own mother. So, when people* *wanted me to do things I didn't want to do, I did it anyway to be accepted, and not feel rejected.*

People Pleasing

My grandmother never thought what I did was good enough. I had to do it perfect. So, I would do things like get good grades just to gain her approval of me. If I did something wrong, I would get punished; in order for me to make up, I learned to be really nice to her like buy her gifts, or do everything perfect so she wouldn't get mad. This explains why I people please, so people can like me and if people get mad at me then I try to make it up by buying gifts or doing things for them that they can do for themselves. I want people to think that I have it going on; but I am a scared little girl and afraid for people to see the real me. I am not the perfect person, I am not strong all the time, and I make mistakes, too.

Confronting Authority (or People)

While growing up with my grandmother she never allowed me to talk about my feelings. She would always shut me down. I learned how to suppress my feelings, I always felt that anybody over me like my boss or my boyfriend, I couldn't disagree with them because I didn't know how to express myself and you don't talk back to your elders, or anyone in authority. This explains why I don't like confronting people because I don't want to be looked at as someone starting trouble or having to be reprimanded, so, I will go along with whatever is going on just to keep the peace. My grandmother was dominating; she liked to be in control and take over. I know for sure that I like to be in control, I like to know what is going on at all times.

Caretaking

My grandmother took care of everybody before she took care of herself. I can take care of people really well and give good advice, but when it comes to taking care of me, I don't do it. I like to rescue and fix people because it gives people a reason to praise me as a good person, a hero. My self-esteem rises whenever I help people. I need people to need me in order for me to be valued as a person, as a human being. This stems from a lack of attention from my parents. Doing for people would get me the attention that I so desired as a child growing up. Instead, of being told I was lazy and didn't want to study, I needed encouragement in a better way than that. This is why I don't take care of me; where does the validation, the praise or the worship come in? Not having boundaries and not knowing when to stop helping others when that behavior became harmful caused me to do for other people to the point where I felt used. But in reality I made it that way because in order for me to be in a relationship I had to be needed.

My Resentment List

Daddy – *For not being there while I was growing up.*

Ernestine – *For giving me up, and when I became grown for not responding when I reached out.*

Uncle – *For violating me as a child, betraying my trust.*

Greg – *For not marrying me, and when I became celibate for tempting me into having sex.*

John – *For not calling me on time to tell me you couldn't go with me to see my mother (and when I arrived at her home, she passed away).*

Trevon – *For not being a husband; always getting high; for leaving me at home by myself; for never being there for me or for us but when you wanted something, you'd come around and be sweet to get what you wanted.*

Myself – *I lied a lot when I was a child so I wouldn't get in trouble, but I still would get a "whupping" whenever I got caught. I am sneaky because I was not able to do the things all that other teens did. I avoid people when I know I've made a decision that isn't good. I want to do what Precious wants to do. I don't like for people to tell me what to do because tall I heard while I was growing up was what I couldn't do, without an explanation. When people try to tell me what to do, I feel like they're controlling me; I don't like to be controlled.*

Jason, *My ex-husband* – *I didn't like the lying, stealing and betrayal. He wasn't there for me because of his drug addiction.*

THE TRUTH HURTS

Beginning to write my Fourth Step was a painful process. I could see the inside of myself and I was discovering my truth. I was self-centered and a selfish individual overall who sought out people, places and things to validate myself because I wasn't equipped with the tools to uplift my own self-esteem. I didn't know my worth as a woman and I didn't think I deserved anything good in my life. I was so distraught by God's revelations about me that all I could do was fall prostrate on the floor and cry. In my mind, I really didn't think I had a problem nor did I think that I played a part in situations that I allowed myself to get caught up in. Hurt, pain and resentment kept me imprisoned which is why I didn't like being by myself. I wasn't content with Precious nor was I comfortable in my own skin. When I was by myself with just my own thoughts, it was overwhelming to think about all of the stuff I had gone through. I didn't know how to process any of it. I always had to be busy with projects or saving, rescuing or attempting to resolve other people's problems to avoid dealing with my own issues. This book exercise was difficult for me because I had to look at the real me and understand that I am not as perfect as I want others to believe. Although this was an agonizing assignment, I now see that I had to be stripped and ripped apart so God could get rid of the stuff that had not allowed me to give and receive real love. I needed to get to the root of the problems that caused me to make wrong choices throughout my life. Also during my self-discovery, I found that I was a scared little girl who made decisions based off fear and I lived my life based on other people's opinions because I didn't trust my own thoughts and ideas. The following day, I decided to take a walk around the Los Angeles Sports Arena parking lot to clear my mind because the night before had drained me mentally and emotionally. As I was walking, I felt like a weight was still on my shoulders and I began to talk to God: *"I feel better about the revelation that was given to me, but I still feel incomplete."* Then God revealed to me the source of my unease: *"You haven't forgiven yourself for allowing people to use and abuse you and you beat yourself up when you make mistakes. Once you forgive yourself then you'll be free."* That night, I wrote a letter in which I forgave myself, and thereafter, God revealed to me that I was forgiven.

5/27/06 – Step 4

Dear God,

Earlier today you revealed to me that I haven't forgiven myself for the situation that I'm in. This letter is to me to start the healing process. I no longer want to be stuck, I want to move forward.

Dear Precious,

I am writing to say I am sorry for neglecting you. I am sorry for not taking care of you like I should have. I've always put other people and things before you. Because I didn't understand why I did what I did you were always last, stepped on, hurt and abused. Today, after 34 years, I now have taken the time to understand me. I am sorry Precious, for taking you through that relationship with Trevon knowing it was unhealthy, but I did so anyway because I wanted Trevon to fix me and fill a void that only God can fill. Once more, I took you through the ringer; everything that I had for myself that God blessed me with, I threw it all away behind needing a man to give me what only God could provide for me: His joy, His peace and His happiness. I am very upset with myself because I am now living with my father when I should be in my own place. Truth be told, I'm Precious Jackson, and I am not supposed to be back at my dad's house. I've worked very hard to become independent. I'm also very upset with myself because I worry about what others will say and think of me for getting a second divorce. I'd rather say that I'm separated than to admit that I'm divorced. I'm worried about my image. Fuck that! I got married for all the wrong reasons, needing to be fixed and to feel connected. I like knowing that I am married and saying it because I want to look good. I always want things to look good from the outside and make people think I have it going on when on the inside everything is all fucked up. I like things to be perfect. I don't like making mistakes because people will look at me as if I did something wrong. These feelings I am experiencing now is how I felt as a child growing up. If I made a mistake I would get into trouble, so that's why I like to be perfect in everything I do. This is crazy, it's like I'm trying to prove to people that I have it together. When I make mistakes in my life I feel ashamed just like I did when I was a child because I felt I let people down. God, I'm asking you tonight to help me to be a person that doesn't beat up on herself when I make a mistake. Help me to recognize why I made them and not to repeat the same mistakes over and over again.

Precious, please forgive me for neglecting you and allowing people to hurt, use and abuse you. Now that I understand where it stems from, I promise I will not allow that to happen again.

Precious Ann Jackson, I love you very much. You are a queen in your own right. You have come a long way and you are not worthless. You are worthy of love and you deserve the best because you were created by the greatest Creator, God. Every morning I want you to say I love you, no matter how you feel that day. As of today, Precious, you are working on yourself and recognizing your part in this situation, and you are seeking a solution to resolve your issues by being willing to play an active part in the solution by speaking and writing about it and praying that you are healed.

God, You didn't say this walk was going to be easy. I'm

cleaning out my house of all the toxins that make my heart and mind sick so that You can fill that void that I have been looking outside of myself to fill. Today, I know the truth. God is the only one who can give me what I need. Goodbye childhood trauma! Hello healing, wholeness, peace, joy and happiness!

Love,

Precious Ann Jackson

O Lord, by these things men live, and in all these things is the life of my spirit: So wilt thou recover me, and make me to live.

Isaiah 38:16

BEAUTIFUL

(When I Started Learning How to Love Myself)

The night I finished writing the letter to myself, I felt free from bondage because I allowed God to do open heart surgery on me and I was a willing vessel. I learned that in order for God to use us the way He wants, we must be stripped of all the 'isms' and baggage that weighs us down through our own emotions. God allowed me to hit rock bottom because He knew that as long as I followed Him, the only place I could go was UP. During my transitional phase I attended City of Refuge Church in Gardena, California and I'd attend two services, sometimes three services, depending on whether or not I needed to stay under the anointing the whole day. I also faithfully went to Bible Study on Wednesday nights and Discipleship class on Sundays before the 6:00 PM *Hour of Power* service. It was in Discipleship class that I developed a deeper relationship with God. There is a difference between knowing God and knowing God for yourself. By that, I mean I had to experience something that man could not provide and only God could pull me through. Without Him, I would not have made it. During Discipleship, we were studying one of my favorite scriptures:

"I am the true vine, and my father is the husbandman. (2) Every branch in me that beareth not fruit he taketh away; and every branch that beareth fruit, he purgeth it, that is may bring forth more fruit. (3) Now ye are clean through the word which I have spoken unto you. (4) Abide in me, and I in you. As the branch cannot bear fruit of itself, except it abide in the vine; no more can ye, except ye abide in me. (5) I am the vine, ye are the branches: He that abideth in me, and I in him, the same bringeth forth much fruit: for without me ye can do nothing. (6) If a man abides not in me, he is cast forth as a branch, and is withered; and men gather them, and cast them into the fire, and they are burned. (7) If ye abide in me, and my words abide in you, ye shall ask what ye will, and it shall be done unto you. (8) Herein is my Father glorified, that ye bear much fruit; so shall ye be my disciples. (9) As the father hath loved me, so have I loved you: continue ye in my love. (10) If ye keep my commandments, ye shall abide in my love; even as I have kept my Father's commandments, and abide in his love. (11) These things have I spoken unto you, that my joy might remain in you, and that your joy might be full. (12) This is my commandment, That ye love one another, as I have loved you. (13) Greater love hath no man than this that a man lay down his life for his friends. (14) Ye are my friends, if ye do whatsoever I command you. (15) Henceforth I call you not servants; for the servant knoweth not what the lord doeth: but I have called you friends; for all things that I have heard of my Father I have made known unto you."

Revelation

(John 15:1-15, King James Version)

I read and meditated on that passage everyday until it was embedded in my soul and I understood it fully. I would say, *"What in the world took you so long to come to Jesus!"* That is what I'd been missing my entire adult life—a relationship with God. He is not only my Lord and Savior, but a friend, someone upon whom I can lean. I can talk to Him any time of day or night. What a true blessing it is to have a friend like Jesus! Once I realized and understood that I needed to always stay connected to the Vine, my life came full circle. I knew what it was like to be lost and I never want to be in that position again. Yes, I still make mistakes and at times I run on self-will but I immediately repent and pray for forgiveness from the Lord and from myself.

LOVING ME: THE GOOD, THE BAD AND THE UGLY

After completing the Fourth Step, I came to accept MYSELF. I wanted to change my perception of Precious A. Jackson and create a new belief system. I began to study the word of God and I could hear His voice in his readings. His words were so profound; He spoke so clearly when He said, *"You are made in my image and everything I make is good."* So, if I'm made from His cloth, then I must be good, right? I meditated on that scripture every day and night and I spoke positive affirmations into existence. I would look in the mirror and tell myself, *"I am beautiful. I am smart. I deserve good things in my life. I deserve nothing but the best. I am lovable. I'm worthy of giving and receiving love and I am made of greatness."* I started to believe what I was saying and once I believed it, my attitude began to change. I felt more confident. I walked with my head held high and my behavior changed. I remember a time when I was still married to Trevon and I was trying to speak words of encouragement to myself. The words had no meaning because I did not like the woman that I saw in the mirror. I needed to take in everything that I had learned and live it wholeheartedly. Each and every aspect of my life had to change, so I made a vow to myself that I would not become involved in a relationship for one year, which meant that I had to practice celibacy to become pure and whole again. I needed to learn how to be in a relationship with myself and to find the inner love that I deserved. So, I kept myself busy and continued to attend CoDA meetings. Those meetings kept me grounded and taught me that I am valuable and important and before I try to fix and repair someone else's life, I must address my own needs. I learned that my personal boundaries protect me from emotional, physical and psychological pain. Setting boundaries and standing firm with them helps me to learn who respects me. When I started saying *"No,"* I would feel guilty because I was so used to giving people my time and saying *"Yes"* just to please them, but I would remind myself that I am the one being used and I would always get the short end of the stick. Those people were fine and they could do for themselves; they had gotten as far as they were without Precious and they were going to have to continue without Precious. Now, it took me a minute to get used to saying *"No,"* but once I said it a few times, the guilt faded and I was at peace.

THE GLOW

Now that everyone's burdens were no longer on my shoulders, I began to feel more confident about my life. I was free. Everything about me exuded my freedom. I had God's glow. I was spiritually filled with His word. People would tell me that there was something different about me. They would ask if I had a new man, which is the question that is asked of every woman in America if she has a new smile on her face and a new twist in her walk. Having a Godly man can enhance a woman's self-esteem and "the glow" is the manifestation. But my glow had nothing to do with Trevon or any other man. For the first time I was taking care of Precious from the inside out.

THE PROPHECY

It's amazing how, when you open your heart and mind to God, everything aligns and blessings begin to come your way. A week after the news special in which I was featured aired on BET I received an email from a guy named Jonathan. I sat at my computer trying to figure out just who this cat was and what he wanted. He explained how he knew me and when I realized who he was I was excited. I started to think back on my life and remembered it vividly: I met Jonathan in 1998 in my African-American History class at Los Angeles Valley Community College. He and I became very good friends. Out of all my friends, Jonathan was the first person that I told about my HIV diagnosis. He never judged me or looked down on me. He encouraged and supported me and that's what made me love our friendship. I didn't return to school the following semester and along the way, we lost contact with one another, but when Jonathan saw me on television, he reached out to me. Jonathan's encouraging words had never left my heart, and when we reconnected, we continued right where we left off. One day Jonathan called me and told me how proud he was of all of the work that I was doing in the community to bring awareness about HIV. He told me that my advocacy will continue to touch lives. I smiled inside because my goal was to inform and teach others, but most importantly to help them live.

"*You know what, Sis? One day you are going to be on The Oprah Winfrey Show,*" Jonathan said. I was like, "*Yeah right,*" but then I knew that if it was God's will, it would happen. Not long after that conversation my co-worker, Araceli called and said, "*Precious! Girl, a producer from the Oprah Winfrey Show left a message for you to call her!*" I was like, "*Girl, stop lying!*" I couldn't believe it! I immediately thought about my brother, Jonathan and gave God some praise. I ran outside to tell my daddy the good news and in the midst of running I stumped my toe on the kitchen chair, but *baaaby*, that didn't stop me. After giving my dad the exciting news, I grabbed my things and headed to the office to return the producer's call. I was filled with joy as I placed that call, but I had to ask the question, "*How did Oprah hear about me?*" The producer informed me that Ms. Winfrey wanted to do a show on HIV and women and in the course of researching the topic, my name came up. She went on to tell me that the show would involve six women who had been diagnosed with HIV—three from the West Coast and three from the East Coast. I was scheduled to fly out of LAX at around 11:30 AM the following Sunday morning.

Before I left for the airport, I attended the 8:00 AM service at City of Refuge. The spirit was heavy as a praise leader uplifted the room. My soul was overtaken by the Holy

Ghost and all I could do was lie on the floor weeping and thanking God for all of the wonderful things that He was sending into my life. To me, there wasn't anything that I felt I was doing to deserve the goodness and mercy that He was bestowing on me. It was by His grace that these doors were opening for me. After leaving church, my best friend, Alfredia drove me to the airport and the beginning of my journey to the Windy City. Once I landed at O'Hare Airport, I went down to the ground transportation area where I saw a man holding a name placard that said *"Precious Jackson."* He took my luggage and escorted me to a black Lincoln Town Car. Normally, whenever I travel I like to take public transportation so I can get the feel of the city, especially on the East Coast when I visit New York or Baltimore but this was Ms. Winfrey's way of showing her hospitality to her guests and boy, did she cater to us. As the driver pulled up to the Omni Hotel I gathered my belongings and the bellhop opened the door to a beautifully designed hotel. The check-in counter was marble and the entire lobby was surrounded by opulent French doors. I was so in awe of my surroundings that when the charming desk clerk began to check me in all I could do was smile. Ms. Winfrey paid for everything including two nights in the hotel; all I had to do was provide a credit card for incidentals. As I was escorted to my room, I began to thank God once again, but when I opened the door, I could feel the blessings still pouring in. Ms. Winfrey had reserved for each of the six women a suite that included a California king sized bed, a 50-inch flat screen television, a bathroom with a sunken tub and marble flooring and countertops, a sitting area for guests and a fully stocked bar. There were bathrobes and slippers available for purchase, but I didn't use them during my stay. Now, when I say that this was an all-expense paid trip, Ms. Winfrey covered everything. Souvenirs and other items were left to us but as far as necessities were concerned, she had that covered. Did I mention that during check-in we received food coupons to cover our breakfast, lunch, snacks and dinner at the hotel? Yes we did! I was able to keep my $100 in my pocket.

The next morning I got up, looked over my itinerary and prepared myself to meet the other five ladies who would be a part of the show. When we first met, we introduced ourselves and were bubbling over with excitement from our invitation to be a part of the *Oprah Winfrey Show*. The car arrived to take us to Harpo Studios where the show was taped in front of a live studio audience. We were greeted by some of the producers and escorted to hair and makeup to prepare for our head shots and blurbs for our stories that would be shown as our introductions to the living room discussion with Oprah. Oprah Winfrey, the queen of talk shows, sat down to interview us ladies. We had an open discussion about our lives, from living with HIV to dating, to stigma, to how we acquired HIV and the importance of taking our medication. We went back to Harpo Studios the following day for the live taping and to our surprise, Magic Johnson and his wife Cookie were also guests on the show. I couldn't believe that I was a part of that experience. To this day, I can still remember those moments and the women who shared their stories on the *Oprah Winfrey Show*. This was an amazing opportunity and I am blessed to have been a part of such an important segment.

EDUCATION IS THE KEY TO OPPORTUNITY

After moving out of my dad's home in June 2007, I fell into the routine of going to work, home, and cozying up on my bed to watch television. I started feeling like my life was at a standstill. I didn't feel like my life was going anywhere and began to feel depressed. One day while channel surfing, a commercial aired for Westwood College. For some reason, the commercial seemed louder than others. It talked about how you could receive your bachelor's degree in three years and how the classes accommodated the schedule of working adults. The Holy Spirit began speaking to me, *"I didn't bring you this far for you to lie around in bed."* I spoke right back. *"You're right God; You didn't bring me this far to do nothing."* I jumped out of bed and looked in the mirror to speak an affirmation onto myself. *"Precious, you are going to school, you are somebody, you are intelligent and you will become a college graduate with a bachelor's degree."* I am so glad that I have the tools to pull from and encourage myself to do things that sometimes require a little push. Without God in my life, I don't know who else would encourage me.

The next day I left work with a little pep in my step as

I headed to Westwood College to enroll. Like any college, you have to speak with a counselor to plan your program and find out what is the best fit for you. After going through a full questionnaire with Mr. Ace, he told me that I was set to go and would be starting school in two weeks. Immediately, I started feeling fear rising. I was mentally prepared to begin school in the spring, but since their school ran on a quarter systems, they didn't have semesters. This allowed people to graduate in three years instead of the traditional four year college program. I gave Mr. Ace all kinds of excuses as to why I couldn't start, like, *"I just moved into my apartment and I still need to get things in order…"* blah, blah, blah, but none of my excuses affected him. He must have been used to adults going through this and I ended up starting in two weeks. Returning to school was one of the best decisions I've ever made. I excelled in school, maintaining a GPA of between 3.5 and 4.0. I really enjoyed college. I knew what I wanted and I was focused. I was able to interact and engage with other working adults who were just as determined to get their degree as I was. I chose the Criminal Justice Bachelor's Degree program because at that time I was working in the jail system and I needed to understand it better. I was taught by some of the best professors who were experts in their field. One professor who comes to mind is Judge Harwin. He was very thorough. What I liked about his class was how he explained laws in detail and gave real life examples of how the law applied. To this very day, I have the notes that I took during his classes. There were some classes I struggled with like Statistics, College Algebra and Physical Science. I had thoughts of giving up, but I kept hearing my grandmother's voice: *"They can take everything from you, but they can't take away your education."* I gave myself pep talks and joined study groups that met on the weekends because of our full time work schedules. Through joining study groups, I was able to understand some of the issues that I was having in classes. I asked a lot of questions and took the lead in solving problems. When the quarter ended for those classes, I had earned all A's. Now, had I not believed in myself and taken the initiative to get help, I would've failed those classes, and knowing me, I would've dropped out of school.

Not only did I learn about the criminal justice system, world history, humanities and earth science, but I also learned that I have a spirit of perseverance that enables me to not give up when obstacles come my way. I had to finish college to prove to myself that I'm smart and that I can accomplish anything I set out to do.

FAMILY REUNION

Several profound events to occur around this time. One night in June 2009 I received a phone call from my little brother Patrick. *"Hey Sis, how you doing Do you know a woman name Ernestine Perry?"* *"No, but I know an Ernestine Gilmore,"* I replied. I heard my little brother say to someone in the background, *"She knows an Ernestine Gilmore."* The person said, *"Yeah, she went by Ernestine Gilmore."* Patrick continued, *"Do you know a Wendy Allen?"* I responded, *"No, but I know a Wendy.* Wendy is one of my older sisters. My other older sister, Phyllis, had died. Patrick then asked me if I knew Donald Allen and I said yes, that Donald Allen was my nephew, Wendy's son. *"Sis, I think I am at your people's house, so, I think you should get here,"* Patrick said. *"I'm on my way,"* I replied.

I was nervous about going to where my brother was, so I asked my friend Nikko to come along. I've known Nikko for 14 years. We started off as friends with benefits, but when that didn't work out, we agreed that it would better to just stay friends without being sexually involved. On the ride to see my brother I had a lot of emotions hitting me at once. I didn't know what I was going to say or who all I would see.

When we pulled up and got out of the car I saw my nephew, Donald who has chocolate smooth skin that glows any time of day.

"What's up, nephew, how you doing?" I asked. *"I'm alright, Auntie,"* Donald replied. *"So, what's this obituary about? Did your mother pass away?"* I asked.

"No, she didn't pass, Auntie, but Grandma passed away last year, on July 2." I was in shock. *"Ernestine—my mother—passed away? Oh, nah! Nah! Nah!"* I responded. *"Yeah, Auntie she passed,"* Donald replied. *"Oh my God! I can't believe she passed away; I didn't get a chance to see her or say goodbye! No wonder I wept for her uncontrollably back in September,"* I said.

The last time I saw my mother was in 2005, before she moved. Both my dad and I had looked for my mother diligently because I wanted to see her before she got sick or passed away. Now, years later, my fears had come to pass. My cries came from within. I had been searching for her since 2005 and now I would never get to say or do the things with and for her that I longed to do. I felt like a lost child wandering in a store trying to find her mother. I felt empty and alone. Tears rolled down my cheeks. Managing to get myself together, I asked my nephew if he could take me to see my younger sister Yvonne. Donald, Nikko and I got in the car and headed over to my sister's house. I just needed to be comforted and wanted to be with my siblings. When we arrived at Yvonne's house, Donald knocked and a guy opened the door. As we walked in, I saw Yvonne sitting in the living room with my niece Janae propped on a pillow doing her hair. My sister looked up: *"Oh my God! Precious Ann! Gurl I've been looking for you, haven't we, Janell?"* Janell, my other niece said, *"Yes, we looked on Myspace and Facebook." "Did you type in Precious Jackson?"* I asked. *"No, we looked under Precious Ann because we didn't know your last name,"* Janell replied.

"Well, no need to look anymore because I'm here in the flesh and I don't ever plan on losing contact with you all again," I responded.

We hugged and cried happy tears because it had been four years since we'd last seen each other. While we were talking a picture of our mother that was sitting on Yvonne's table fell. Mind you, we are in the house without any windows open and her picture fell. We both looked at each other and said, *"Mama's spirit is here."* We took that as a sign that she was happy that her child had reconnected with her family and her picture hasn't fallen since that moment. Sitting and talking with my sister, I learned something that knocked my socks off: Yvonne and our mother had been living on Yukon and 104th in Inglewood in 2007 when I lived right down the street on 104th and Darby. This world is big and small at the same time. Unfortunately, our mother went into a diabetic coma and died at Centinela Hospital in Inglewood. The bright side of it all was that I reconnected with my big brother, Richard, my oldest sister, Wendy and my nieces, nephews and cousins whom I had never met. I kept my promise to them and we're still connected.

From the right: My sisters Wendy, center Yolanda,
my niece Jada, my nephew Kenny & my nephew Ronald

mile-stone (mīl stōn)

(noun): A significant event or stage in life, progress, development, or the like of the person, nation, etc.

I did it! On May 26, 2011, I graduated from college with a Bachelor of Science degree. I was in tears during the entire ceremony because I'm the first college graduate on both my mother and my father's side of the family. This was truly a milestone. Yvonne and I coordinated my graduation party because not only did I want to celebrate my accomplishment, but to recognize those who encouraged, inspired and provided hope to help me along my journey. Having an education provides access to opportunities to walk through doors, but it is up to you to promote and sell yourself.

A mind is a terrible thing to waste.

– United Negro College Fund

My dad Percy Jackson & me
Graduation picture from 2011

OPPORTUNITY OF
A LIFETIME

In September 2007, I attended the United States Conference on AIDS in Palm Springs, CA. I was sitting in the lobby during happy hour having some cocktails with friends when I heard someone call my name. I looked over and it was the diva herself, Ms. Sheryl Lee Ralph, the founder of the DIVA Foundation. I was shocked that she remembered me from being an employee at Women Alive. Since the last time I saw her, I had transitioned to the Center for Health Justice doing HIV prevention work in the Los Angeles County Jail System. I walked over to greet Ms. Ralph and we discussed the Sister Circle, a project that the DIVA Foundation was working on. It consisted of twenty-five American women of African descent who would travel to Cape Town, South Africa as delegates to a women's conference. The purpose was to connect with other women living with or affected by HIV by showing them that we are all alike.

I was at work when I received an email from the DIVA Foundation. I opened the attached letter that stated, *"You have been invited to participate in the Sister Circle."* I couldn't believe my eyes. Sheryl Lee Ralph was really serious about me participating in this project. I responded to the email letting them know that I was humbled and honored to have been selected to be a part of that initiative and that I would be more than happy to participate. The letter also asked if I could secure a sponsorship from the agency to cover airfare and lodging. I discussed the trip with the Executive Director of the Center for Health Justice and asked if the agency could sponsor me. Unfortunately, the agency couldn't justify the expenditure from the grant from which I was being paid to conduct women's empowerment classes with a focus on HIV prevention as falling within the scope of my work. I was disappointed because this was an opportunity of a lifetime. I emailed the DIVA Foundation to inform them that I would not be able to attend. A few hours later, I received a call from Ms. Ralph inquiring as to why I couldn't participate. I informed her of the situation with my job. She asked me if I really wanted to go and I said, *"Yes, I've always wanted to go to Africa and I didn't care which country.* I prayed to God: *"If it is in Your will, I want to be a participant in this meaningful event."* That same week I received a call from Ms. Ralph's assistant stating that they were able to secure sponsorships for some of the participants and I was one of them. I damn near jumped out of my chair when I heard the news that I would be able to attend. I thanked and praised God for answering my prayers. We would be traveling to Cape Town, South Africa and staying for one week and one day. I reflected over the changes that had taken place in my life. Had I not had the courage to leave Trevon in February 2006, where would I be? I probably would have been cracked out or lost my mind and wouldn't have had the opportunity to experience the abundance of blessings God has bestowed upon me. This is what we call Grace—free or undeserved favor from God.

I was excited and nervous at the same time because the flight was 17 hours and in another country. I didn't know what to expect. In my distorted mind, like most people, I envisioned Africa as nothing but jungle and indigenous people living in huts in their villages, wearing tribal attire. I was sadly mistaken. When we began to descend into Johannesburg, where we were to take a connecting flight into Cape Town, tears flowed down my face. I couldn't believe that I was about to step onto the soil on which my ancestors walked. When we got off the plane we were greeted by the South African Airline staff saying, *"Welcome home, my sistah."* I started crying again and praising God for allowing me to land safely and for giving me this opportunity to be amongst the people from which I descended.

We were lodged in an exquisite hotel. It was nothing that I would have imagined. We were housed four women to a condominium and I had the pleasure of rooming with the first black woman to publicly disclose her HIV status in *Essence* magazine. I was in awe of her act of courage in sharing her story during a time when no one wanted to be around people who were infected with HIV or AIDS. If you think stigma is something now, even with so much information at our fingertips, it was horrendous then. That evening we all gathered in the lobby area to be welcomed by the DIVA Foundation and its collaborative partners that made the trip possible. It was so emotional; there wasn't a dry eye in the room. When it was my turn to speak I was so filled with emotion I couldn't help but holla, *"Thank you, Jesus, thank you, Jesus, oh Lord I just thank you!"* The Holy Ghost hit me and I went in.

The conference began the next day in a township called Gugulethu. It was held at a church that served as a mission and lasted three days. As we entered, we were greeted with an amazing song sung by local participants who harmonized beautifully. The pastor opened the conference by welcoming us to the country. They were excited to have us. It felt really good to be around my people; I felt connected. The first day consisted of empowering and motivating speeches from community activists and dignitaries. The mission had several HIV prevention programs where some of the staff, along with clients living with HIV had written a skit about stigma in their township and how it perpetuated the spread of the disease in their communities. The neat thing about it was that some of the clients were cast members which hit home for a lot of the men and women at risk of or living with HIV. They used this skit as a tool to inform the community of the importance of getting educated, tested and involved in stopping the transmission and acquisition of HIV. When the skit ended the floor was opened for questions and answers. One of the questions was how many people had been impacted by the play. They said they'd had an overwhelmingly positive response from people who asked questions about HIV and an increase in the number of people who had begun to use HIV testing and using condoms.

As the first day winded down, we had the opportunity to socialize with South African women who came from the townships. For me, that was one of the highlights of the trip. I was asked what it was like to live in America; what kind of music I listened to; how I felt when I found out I was HIV positive; if I had children and if not whether I wanted to have children. In response to my questions, I learned that South Africans have to pay to go to primary school which made me ever so grateful for the opportunities that some of us take for granted or don't take advantage of. Some households didn't have running water or electricity unless it was jimmy rigged. If you've seen depictions of tin roof shacks in the Black townships it is still like that in most parts of South Africa today. You haven't seen poverty until you've been outside of the United States. I said to myself, if I ever complain about what I don't have I want God to cause me to recall the South African townships.

On the second day, we had the opportunity to hear some of the women's and men's stories. There were two in particular that stand out in my mind. The first is the story of a young lady who acquired HIV after being gang raped. Some African men believe that if they have sex with a young girl they will be cured of HIV. The lady had the courage to report the crime to the police and the men were arrested and convicted. Since then, she has made a commitment to advocate for women and girls who are infected and affected by HIV and to be the voice for the voiceless. This young lady's story was compelling because she took back her power and did not sing a victim song. The other story that brought tears to my eyes was about a young man who was in attendance with his wife. Both of them were HIV infected. The husband acquired HIV from a gang rape while he was in the military. Not only was he raped, but he was tortured as well. By the grace of God, he managed to escape to his village only to find both of his parents were no longer living. He'd never told his story publicly until that day at the conference. When he finished he received a standing ovation. It is not often that you find a heterosexual male who is HIV positive and open about his status.

On the third day, it was our turn to tell our stories. Once again there wasn't a dry eye in the church. Our African sisters responded, saying they were inspired, appreciative and honored to have us in their space. Then a lady stood up and began to sing. Our African sisters joined in, singing in their native tongue. It was the most beautiful thing I'd ever heard. Mind you, they didn't have any instruments; this is what we call right off the cuff. As the tears rolled down my face, I thought about how magnificent we are. I also had a better understanding of who we are as a people, our resilience to continue to move forward when we don't have much, our ability to rise above circumstances brought on by external forces, and our strong faith in God. When the ladies finished singing we gave them a standing ovation, and in return, we sang the Black National Anthem, *Lift Every Voice and Sing*. The conference was amazing. I got to interact with my people and developed the understanding that we're more similar than different. What I've discovered that still holds true today is that the powers that be continue to spread propaganda that Blacks in America are inferior, not to be trusted, lazy and only want to collect a welfare check. If you've ever interacted with an African from, say, Nigeria and noticed their attitude toward Americans of African descent, they have a proclivity to think that they're superior to us. What they fail to realize is that they are perpetuating divisiveness between us and them when in fact, we're all in the same boat. When you understand institutionalized racism and how it affects us domestically and internationally then you don't hate the people, you hate the system. The Willie Lynch syndrome is alive and well, honey, even though it was implemented over 200 years ago.

We ended the day with dinner at an exquisite restaurant. Our African sistahs were invited also. The restaurant was under a tent with beautiful tropical plants and the servers were dressed in tribal attire. The food was set up buffet style. It was unbelievable—everything from chicken, goat, and lamb to a variety of salads and side dishes. I ate until I couldn't eat anymore. They also had a live show where men and women from different tribes danced and then they opened up the dance floor for the guests. I love to dance, so I got up and got my party on. I really enjoyed myself. When we dropped the ladies off in their townships, they sang a song and did a tribal dance. I was moved and once again brought to tears.

The last four days of our trip consisted of pre-planned tourist attractions. We visited Robben Island where Nelson Mandela was imprisoned for over 25 years which is now a museum. It's heartbreaking to know that Mr. Mandela and his comrades were imprisoned for fighting a system of injustice and inequality. We also visited an AIDS organization whose mission is to empower women through jewelry making which in turn helps them to gain financial stability from its sale in the agency's jewelry boutique. While there, we had another opportunity to socialize and network with other women who were living with HIV. As I was standing outside of the jewelry boutique with some ladies, a young man who was passing by turned around and asked if I had been on the *Oprah Winfrey Show*. I teased with him for a few minutes pretending that it wasn't me, but then I soon let him know that it was me. OMG! I was shocked that someone recognized me from 10,000 miles away. I was in awe of how amazing God was and still is. I hope my story has had an impact and if so, then my mission was accomplished. I took a picture with him but unfortunately, I lost my camera four years ago. It contained all of the pictures I'd taken while I was in Cape Town. The only proof I have that I've been to South Africa is some money and handmade jewelry I brought back. Definitely, a big lesson learned is to save all of my pictures on my computer. Now that technology is advanced, I save everything onto my Google Drive.

top left: Fertility dolls
top right: South African jewelry
bottom photo: South African money (Rand)

MY FIRST LOVE

God has a way of getting what He wants from us. When I moved back in with my dad the second time around, God told me that I needed to forgive and repair my relationship with my father. I walked into the kitchen one day where my daddy was piddling around. *"Daddy can we talk,"* I said. *"Sure baby, what do you want to talk about?"* he replied. *"So, daddy I am writing a resentment list of everyone who has ever hurt me in the past and I added you to my list."* I said. *"Hmm….go on,"* he said. *"Daddy, I carried a lot of hurt and resentment for a long time because you weren't present during my adolescent years, when I really needed you the most. I don't know if you ever noticed during my teenage and young adult years how I disrespected you,"* I continued. *"Yeah, I noticed there was something wrong, but I didn't know what,"* my dad said. *"I believe because you weren't present I made poor choices when it came to men; I was seeking love and attention which led me to allow other men to take advantage of me. I realized that I chose men whose attitudes emulated yours,"* I replied.

My dad was a pimp, a hustler and a dope fiend who was heavily involved in the streets. I can remember a time when my father and some dude were arguing in front of my grandmother's house. My dad was telling the guy to give him his money and the guy responded with a few words that got under his skin. My father went to the back of his truck and grabbed a big stick and chased the man down the street. At that moment, I decided that I wanted a man just like my daddy because he wasn't a punk. When my dad was around, I could talk to him about boys and he would give me sound advice, but because I was angry with my dad I allowed it to go in one ear and right out the other. And when I went against his advice and experienced what he said what would happen, I was like, *"Damn, my daddy was right, I think I better listen to him next time,"* but I wouldn't dare tell him he was right; my pride would not allow me to because of my stubbornness. My dad said, *"Baby, I love you to the core and during that time I was caught up in my addiction, the streets. That street mentality would not allow me to be there for you like I should have been. I wanted more than anything to be the father that you wanted me to be, but my addiction would not allow it. It was easier for me to take you to your grandmother's house because the streets were not a place to raise a child. Can you or will you ever forgive me?"* he asked. "Yes, daddy, I forgive you and would you forgive me for disrespecting you all of those years?" *"Yes,"* he replied, as and we gave each other a big hug.

There was a sigh of relief because I got my daddy back. On the "Daddyless Daughters" segment of *Oprah's Life Class,* Iyanla Vanzant eloquently stated, *"Daddies teach their girls how to have a non-sexual relationship with a man, daddies give their girls confidence, boost their self-esteem and teach them to be secure in their womanhood."* That's exactly what my daddy taught me at the age of 35. I've always been a Daddy's Girl and I can remember when I was little that I was always with my daddy up until I was 14; that's when I noticed he wasn't coming around as much, but when he did come around I could talk to him about any and everything. my dad was the type of man to keep an open line of communication with all of his children.

Since reconciling with my dad, we spent a lot of time together laughing, talking and going to dinner, church, social gatherings and spending quality time at his home. We were able to build the father-daughter relationship that I had always desired. My dad had been clean and sober for six years. During that time, he turned his life around and re-committed his life to Christ. He became an active Deacon of Mt. Arron Christian Center in Los Angeles. He had a loving spirit and could strike up a conversation with anyone. My dad had a heart of gold and if he could help you in any way, he would. Whenever anyone met my father they would say, *"Your dad is amazing! He has a welcoming and approachable spirit."* My dad was very handsome, and I would tease him all the time. *"Daddy, you got it going on; you can still pull the women with your oxygen tank on."* He would laugh and say, *"Girl, hush."* Not a day went by that I didn't talk to my father or go by his house to see him.

One morning in October 2013, I called my dad to check in and he told me he was coughing up blood. I told him he needed to go to the doctor to get checked out. When my dad told me that my heart dropped because I had a feeling he had terminal lung cancer. My mommy Georgette had the same exact symptoms when she was diagnosed with terminal lung cancer in July 2003 and she made her transition in March 2004. Unfortunately, both my mother and daddy smoked cigarettes back in the day. So, my dad made an appointment with his doctor and informed the doctor of his symptoms. The doctor ordered a chest x-ray which was done the same day. When the results came back Nancy, the medical assistant called me and said, *"Dr. Anthony would like for you to come in with your father for his results; are you available?"* Baby, I knew then something was wrong because Dr. Anthony never requested that I come with my dad to his appointments; I just made it made a point to go with him so I could keep up with his health. I immediately went into prayer asking God to heal my dad's body. The next day my dad and I went to his appointment. Dr. Anthony asked how my dad was doing and cut straight to the chase. The results from the chest X-Rays showed a mass on his right upper lung; when I heard that, I had to leave the room because I didn't want my dad to see me crying. I knew in my spirit he had terminal stage 4 lung cancer. I had gotten myself together and went back into the room. I had never met a doctor like Dr. Anthony before.

When I first met Dr. Anthony he made it known that he was a believer in Jesus Christ and that he was just a vessel that God uses. Dr. Anthony said that the mass was small, but he didn't want to wait to treat it, so he would be treating it like it was cancer. He referred us to an oncologist for additional testing. *"I believe in the power of prayer and we're going to pray for the healing of the mass in the right upper lung,"* Dr. Anthony said.

When we left the doctor's office, I asked my dad how he felt about what was said. *"I'm not claiming cancer at all,"* he said, but I could tell from his body language that he was worried. The next few months I noticed how my dad was starting to forget things more than usual which I attributed to the amount of stress he was under. I would call him two or three times just to make sure he didn't forget what he needed to do that day. One day, he called and told me he forgot how to get to my brother, Michael's house, and he said he felt scared and confused. I told my dad if he felt that way then he needed to stop driving and start using Access transportation. He put up a fuss, but realized it was best for him because he didn't want to become a danger to himself and others. Since I worked during the day, my brother would check on him, take him to run his errands and when I got off, I would take him out for dinner and bring him back home.

Things took a turn for the worse on December 26, 2013. My dad was still coughing up blood and we had yet to receive the referral to see the oncologist. My father's breathing was abnormal and I had to call an ambulance. He was agitated at the thought of the paramedics coming, but his best friend helped to persuade him that it was for the best. Once the paramedics arrived they took my father's vitals and checked his oxygen level, which was very low. After arriving at the hospital emergency room, we spent one day and night there waiting for my dad to be transferred and admitted into California Hospital so he could be seen by a pulmonary and brain specialist. The emergency room physician informed me that from the looks of the MRI, my father had developed a mass on the right side of his brain as well. I called my brother, Michael, to inform him of daddy's condition. At that time Michael was in Atlanta visiting our sister for the holidays. He told me not to worry and that he would be leaving Atlanta on Friday and he would be back in Los Angeles on Sunday. My dad had a phobia about being in hospitals. He would have the nurses call me and I would have to reassure him that he needed to be there to get better. Between my brother and sister calling daddy, I felt a weight had been lifted off my shoulders because I had a support system.

On Friday, December 27th I went to back to the hospital to check on daddy. Both the pulmonary and the brain doctor were on the floor. They ran a CAT scan, an MRI and additional tests. The brain doctor talked to me first. He showed me the results from both tests. The mass on my dad's brain had gotten bigger and had spread to his liver. *"Your father has stage four terminal lung cancer. If we do any type of treatment, it could tire his body out,"* the specialist said.

The tumor on his brain explained why my dad had become so forgetful. After receiving one cluster of news, the pulmonary doctor told me that with the combination of Chronic Obstructive Pulmonary Disease (COPD) and the cancer in my father's lungs, he didn't have much time to live. He advised me to make arrangements for my dad to be placed in hospice as he wouldn't have a poor life in a hospital hooked up to tubes and ventilators. Tears welled up in my eyes. The thing I feared most had come to past. My daddy was dying and my emotions were out of control. I was fucked up. I walked back into the room with my daddy and spent a few more hours with him before I left to go home.

I called my brother and sister to inform them of the news. By this time, Michael was on the road coming back home to Los Angeles and he was devastated. He told me to try to be strong for dad until he got back home. I told him that it would be difficult, but I would try. I just sat in my car and cried like a baby thinking, *"Damn, I'm about to lose my daddy and I'll be all alone because all of the women who had a part in raising me are deceased."* It was a scary place to be, emotionally and mentally, but I thank God that He kept my mind intact. My friends Alfredia, Rachel, Monica, Cynthia and Kim were there for me every step of the way. Michael talked to daddy at least three times a day while he was on the road coming back home and each time daddy talked to Michael he would say, *"Son, when you coming to take me home, I'm ready to get out of this hospital. I keep telling Precious I need to get out of here, but she isn't listening to me."* I would just shake my head and attempt to soothe him by telling him that once he got better that the doctor would discharge him. Since the time my daddy was admitted into the hospital in El Monte and transferred to California Hospital I didn't miss a day going to see him.

On Sunday evening, when Michael arrived at the hospital my dad's face lit up like a kid in a candy store. He had this big Kool-Aid smile on his face as they gave each other a hug. I brought Michael up to speed about daddy's condition and we both spoke with the oncologist that evening about the test results. The doctor informed us that our father would have two months to live, if that. The cancer started in his lungs and spread to his brain and then to his liver. My father had so many lesions on his liver that the doctor stopped counting after thirty. When Michael heard for himself how bad off daddy was he did a good job of masking it in front of him, but when we left to go home he was very emotional and said, *"Sis, you know I got to have a drink tonight because I'm fucked up! I'm about to lose my pop!"* We gave each other a big hug and I went home crying my eyes out.

Daddy was discharged from the hospital the next day. On Monday, December 30th, Michael picked up our father from the hospital and we both agreed that my dad and I would stay at his house so that we could care for him. Michael worked nights, so during the daytime while I was at work he would be there with dad and when I got off I would take over. It took some adjusting because I went from living alone to a full house of two nieces, a nephew and a sister-in-law. It's times like these when your family is either going to come together or fall to pieces. Luckily, we came together as a unit for the care of our father. I truly thank God I went through the process of forgiving my dad and rebuilding our relationship. If we hadn't, I probably would not have been able to set aside all of the hurt and pain to be an asset during my father's illness. Life is too short to hold on to hurt, pain and disappointment; all it does is hurt you in the long run. While you're mad at the person who offended you; you're missing out on things that matter and that person has gone about their business enjoying life. If you're reading this book and you haven't spoken to your parents because of what they did or didn't do, forgive them of their shortcomings; let it go and mend your relationship. When the day comes for them to transition, it will be too late and you don't want to have any I *coulda, woulda, shoulda* regrets.

It was very difficult to see my father decline rapidly. He went from being able to walk, put on his own clothes, and feed himself to not walking at all. I was an emotional wreck. I'd often break down and cry at work and my co-workers, Jennifer and Edwin were really awesome in supporting me through that challenging time. I'm truly grateful for my supervisors, Angel and Erin for understanding the situation with my family and allowing me to take the time off that I needed.

While my father's health was failing he managed to keep up a hefty appetite until the week of February 17th. Michael and I noticed that he started to eat less which we had been told by the hospice nurse would happen. On Sunday, February 23, 2014, I went to church and Michael was at home when the nurse from Rose Room Hospice Care came to do her routine checkup on daddy. When I came home I asked my brother, *"What did the nurse say about daddy?" "Presh, it's not looking good. He's starting to make his transition,"* he replied. I started crying and so did Michael. After getting myself together, I went into the room where my daddy and I slept.

He was lying in a peaceful state. I kissed him on his forehead and I talked to him. He responded by saying, "Hmmm," because he was no longer able to talk.

I woke up the next morning, Monday, February 24, 2014 at 5:30 AM holding my daddy's hand. Before I got up I said the Lord's Prayer and daddy tried to mumble along with me, but nothing came out. All he could say was *"Hmmm"* and that which was good enough for me. Before my dad stopped talking the brain tumor caused him to lose short term memory, but his long term memory was still intact. In fact, he remembered the Lord's Prayer and although he couldn't verbalize it he made noises to let me know he could hear me.

I debated with myself if I should go to work or not. I wanted to be by his side if he passed because I felt in my spirit that he would be making his transition soon. I decided to go into work so I could try to get my mind off my dad for a minute. My spirit was very low and I couldn't concentrate. I remember walking around in a fog. I called Michael to check on daddy and the nurse was there again since he was in the transitioning phase. After being in the office for four hours it was time for me to conduct a home visit with my client. The visit went very well.

Michael called me at 1:30 PM as I was on my way back to the office. He didn't sound good. He said, *"Presh, Dad is gone!"* I replied, *"What, he's gone! Oh, my God! Daddy passed away, Big Brother?"* I told my brother to just give me a minute because I was coming from Pasadena but I was on my way home. I was so frantic that I had to pull over so I wouldn't hit anyone. I managed to text my supervisors through the tears to inform them I wasn't coming back to the office, my dad had just passed away.

I'm so thankful that I took heed to God's order to get my relationship right with my daddy. Because I was obedient to God's words my daddy and I were inseparable until he took his last breath on the afternoon of Monday, February 24th. My friends in my inner circle knew that I loved my daddy like a fat kid loves cake. I love and miss you so much daddy! There isn't a day that goes by that I don't think about you.

Daddy has now joined his mother, Dessie Mae Jackson-Randolph (Big Mama), his father, Robert Lee Jackson (Papa), my mother, Ernestine Gilmore-Perry (Mama) and my other mother who raised me, Georgette Harrison (Mommy) all of whom are in heaven rejoicing every day, now and forever, Amen.

My Dad & me, May 2010

A BOND THAT CAN'T BE BROKEN

I always had a good relationship with my older brother, Michael L. Jackson, but when our dad became terminally ill it made our bond that much stronger. I've always admired and looked to Michael because he is the epitome of a big brother. Whenever I got into it with any of my former boyfriends, Michael and my dad would be right there to rescue me, or if any of his friends tried to holla at me, he would block all actions. Not only did he protect me, but Michael has always given me sound advice. God has blessed my brother with a beautiful wife and six beautiful children and one step daughter, all of whom he loves dearly and they love him, too. I'm truly grateful for my sister-in-law, Trisha, for being on one accord with her husband and opening up their home for Mike and me to take care of our father.

What I've learned about my brother is that he has a big heart; Michael will give you the shirt off his back, and when his family needs him, he's there asking, *"What do you need me to do?"* My brother has been called to serve and he does so with compassion, patience and a genuine concern to see that people are treated with dignity and respect. I'm truly grateful for my brother's love and guidance and this is a bond that can never be broken. I love you Big Brother. Thank you for being here!

My brother Michael & me, May 2014

EPILOGUE

For a long time I was reluctant to write this book because I was fearful of what people would think of me outside of being this great national HIV prevention advocate. I found it very easy to disclose my HIV status, but when it came to talking about other struggles that I've gone through it was difficult. People would constantly say, *"Precious, you need to write a book, you have a helluva story."* I wasn't ready and willing to bear my soul at that time. Several years ago I was at church and Pastor Joe was preaching about not letting your dreams die: *"Some people have a book in them, some have a business to develop, and some people have a film in them,"* he said. I felt a tugging in my spirit when he mentioned writing a book. I knew then that God was telling me it's time to tell the world how He brought me out of my mess but I still wasn't ready. God kept tugging at my spirit to write my book, but I allowed fear of judgment from others to keep me from moving forward. It wasn't until March 2013 when I was having a conversation with my friend Corey about life and the things we went through and how we were able to recover and heal, that it hit me: There are some women who need to know that you don't have to have been a drug addict to be FULL FLIGHT FROM REALITY—to make irrational decisions and to become emotionally, spiritually and physically bankrupt. That Sunday night, I began to write my story. Later, when I heard Pastor Rick Warren, author of *The Purpose Driven Life* say on *Oprah's Life Class* that, *"Your life is not your own; it belongs to God for Him to as He will for His purpose,"* tears rolled down my eyes. I surrendered and said, *"Yes, Lord I heard you"* and God confirmed that I was on the right path. So, here I am, a year and a half later, with a finished book, *Revelation: Unveiling the Mask*. I pray that this book will have an impact on people's lives. We sometimes create our own chaos by the decisions we make, but our lives don't have to remain chaotic. We have the choice to learn the lesson and get the blessing or to remain stuck and play the victim role. Today, I am a recovered co-dependent. I no longer have the desire to try to fix or rescue anyone. My life is drama-free, serene, and full. God has given us power and authority over our lives, so let's use our God-given gift and LIVE!

Me, May 2014

About the Author

Precious A. Jackson was born and raised in South Los Angeles during a time when social prejudices were very relevant, she relied on the values instilled in her as a child and became an independent college graduate who reached back to lend a helping hand within her community. Teaching others to pay it forward became her motivation until she was taken on an emotional roller coaster ride when her doctor delivered the devastating news that she tested positive for HIV.

Not giving strength to her diagnosis, Precious knew what her next mission would be: to educate both men and women equally on the importance of getting tested and protecting themselves at all cost. Adamant about bringing awareness to everyone, Precious has been featured in the *Los Angeles Times, Washington Post, The Oprah Winfrey Show, BET News Special* and *Newsweek, Essence* and *Ebony*. In 2008, she was given the opportunity to travel to Cape Town, South Africa with *Sheryl Lee Ralph's Sister Circle*, a program of the Diva Foundation that helps to create a global connection and movement with other women whom were infected with HIV.

Today, Precious is empowering others to be courageous in announcing they are beautiful and helps them face their battles of self-esteem issues. Receiving the Social Service Provider Award from the Los Angeles County Women's HIV/AIDS Task Force and a certification as a HIV Testing Counselor and Hepatitis C Community Educator's trainer, Precious is always delving into the lives of others to help them survive.